Six String Journal

Classical Guitar Technique Series

Mastering Diatonic Scale Forms

By Leonardo Garcia

Six String Journal

Classical Guitar Technique Series

Mastering Diatonic Scale Forms

By Leonardo Garcia

MASTERING DIATONIC SCALE FORMS

Scale mastery is absolutely essential for the ambitious and serious guitarist. Touted as the single most effective way to solve technical problems by the most distinguished pedagogues and professionals, developing a scale practice and understanding the most useful way to develop it will lead to breakthroughs and improvement in your technique. Mastering Diatonic Scale Forms is geared towards the advancing guitarist and offers a practical approach for understanding the various necessary scale forms and some insightful methods to supercharge the results of your study.

Use the practice journal at the end of this book to record your progress with reflections, note which movements are more difficult or more comfortable, and keep track of tempo. This process is all about self-discovery.

Good luck!

For Max and Charlie

Table of Contents

Preparatory Exercises for Scales

The following preparatory exercises focus on the building blocks for the successful execution of scales: finger alternation, string crossing, left- and right-hand finger coordination, and shifts. Practicing these exercises will build a solid foundation of endurance and coordination and will facilitate the technical aspect of playing scales.

Focus on the following key points:

1) Practice perfect alternation – As the finger performing the stroke moves toward its resting point, the next finger should release from its resting point to prepare the next stroke.

2) Keep everything relaxed – The energy is in the stroke; once it is performed, the finger should release all energy and tension. In the best-case scenario, the tension of the finger is released as the alternating finger exerts energy on the next stroke.

3) If you are still developing a technical base, spend more time on the basics – *im, ma, ia,* and finger alternation with *p* are the most important fingerings to develop, as all the others contain these basic movements.

Spend as much time as necessary within each step or rhythm to achieve improved tone consistency, stroke efficiency, rhythmic precision, and perhaps speed (although speed will result from developing the former aspects). Use the third string as a starting point before exploring other strings. If your nails wear easily, protect them with packing tape, or keep most of your practice relegated to the first three strings. And, of course, don't forget to use your friend the metronome.

Finger Alternation

Though not exhaustive, the following three exercises provide a simple and unencumbered way to focus on one of the most important foundational skills for playing guitar well. Use them to focus on efficient and relaxed alternation, tone, consistency, and rhythmic pulse. More advanced students could expand them with articulations such as staccato and legato, dynamics, and tempo. Practice the material between repeats more than twice when necessary.

Rest-stroke fingerings: *im, mi, ma, am, ia, ai, p, ami, ima, imam, amim, aimi*
Free-stroke fingerings: *im, mi, ma, am, ia, ai, pi, pm, pa, ami, ima, imam, amim, aimi, pmi, pami*

Exercise 1

Exercise 2

Exercise 3

String Crossing

The first four essential string-crossing movements are categorized into descending (from string 1 to string 6) and ascending (from string 6 to string 1). For each, practice the efficient movements given (*i* crosses first) before the less efficient ones.

Rest-stroke fingerings: *im, ma, ia (and the alternate less efficient patterns mi, am, ai)*
Free-stroke fingerings: *im, ma, ia, pi, pm, pa (and the alternate less efficient patterns mi, am, ai, ip, mp, ap)*

Exercise 1

Exercise 2

Rest-stroke fingerings: *mi, am, ai (and the alternate less efficient patterns im, ma, ia)*
Free-stroke fingerings: *mi, am, ai, ip, mp, ap (and the alternate less efficient patterns im, ma, ia, pi, pm, pa)*

Exercise 3

Exercise 4

To develop a more flexible and nimble string-crossing technique, apply the following right-hand fingerings to Exercises 1–4 and to Exercises 5 and 6 below.

Rest-stroke fingerings: *im, mi, ma, am, ia, ai, p, ami, ima, imam, amim, aimi*
Free-stroke fingerings: *im, mi, ma, am, ia, ai, pi, pm, pa, ami, ima, imam, amim, aimi, pmi, pami*

Exercise 5

Exercise 6

Right- and Left-Hand Finger Coordination

Right- and left-hand finger coordination is ultimately developed through scale practice, but keep in mind that both hands already prefer to act together in a coordinated fashion. It is useful to develop this natural coordination further, but it is actually the counter-coordination that requires some practice to fully realize finger independence. Therefore, the construction of simple coordination exercises involves left-hand groups of 2, 3, and 4 finger movements with right-hand fingerings.

An example of a movement with natural coordination would be a left-hand movement of finger 1 to finger 2 plucked with right-hand fingers *i* and *m*. In other words, both index fingers act together, followed by a movement where both middle fingers act together. Or another way to think of it is that the finger movements in each hand are both directionally moving toward the finger 4 (pinky) side of the hand.

An example of a movement with counter-coordination would be a left-hand movement of finger 1 to finger 2 plucked with right-hand fingers *m* and *i*. Here, the finger movements in the hands are moving in the opposite direction: the left-hand fingers move toward finger 4 (pinky) while the right-hand fingers move toward the thumb.

Practice the following basic natural and counter-coordination movements starting on C on string 3 (fret 5). Explore these in various positions. I prefer to use the non-wound strings to minimize nail wear. Numbers correspond to left-hand fingers (1=index, 2=middle, 3=ring, 4=pinky).

Exercise 1 – Two Finger Movements

Natural Coordination

12, 23, 34, 13, 24, 14 paired with *im, ma, ia* (use rest and free stroke)
21, 32, 43, 31, 42, 41 paired with *mi, am, ai* (use rest and free stroke)

Counter-Coordination

12, 23, 34, 13, 24, 14 paired with *mi, am, ai* (use rest and free stroke)
21, 32, 43, 31, 42, 41 paired with *im, ma, ia* (use rest and free stroke)

Exercise 2 – Three Finger Movements

Natural Coordination

123, 234, 134, 124 paired with *ima* (use rest and free stroke)
321, 432, 431, 421 paired with *ami* (use rest and free stroke)

Counter-Coordination

123, 234, 134, 124 paired with *ami* (use rest and free stroke)
321, 432, 431, 421 paired with *ima* (use rest and free stroke)

Exercise 3 – Four Finger Movements

Natural Coordination

1234 paired with *imim, mama, iaia* (use rest and free stroke)
4321 paired with *mimi, amam, aiai* (use rest and free stroke)

Counter-Coordination

1234 paired with *mimi, amam, aiai* (use rest and free stroke)
4321 paired with *imim, mama, iaia* (use rest and free stroke)

Exercise 4 – Three Finger with Two Finger Movements

Natural and Counter-Coordination

123, 234, 134, 124 paired with *im, ma, ia, mi, am, ai* (use rest and free stroke)
321, 432, 431, 421 paired with *im, ma, ia, mi, am, ai* (use rest and free stroke)

Exercise 5 – Two Finger with Three Finger Movements

Natural and Counter-Coordination

12, 23, 34, 13, 24, 14 paired with *ima* (use rest and free stroke)
21, 32, 43, 31, 42, 41 paired with *ami* (use rest and free stroke)
(i.e., play 12 repeatedly 121212... while using *imaimaima...*)

Exercise 6 – Four Finger with Three Finger Movements

Natural and Counter-Coordination

1234 paired with *ami and ima* (use rest and free stroke)
4321 paired with *ima and ami* (use rest and free stroke)

Pairing the right-hand fingerings above with a combination of patterns is another useful way to develop coordination:

Exercise 6 – Complex Movements

Due to the near infinite number of potential coordination patterns, this section may seem overwhelming—but its purpose is to help identify coordination issues that can then be isolated and further developed, either through the practice of the movements above or through scales themselves.

Shifts

Shifts are another necessary technical component of left-hand technique applicable to scales. The key points to remember when shifting positions are:

1. Relax the tension of the left hand while remaining in contact with at least one guide finger.
2. Left-hand thumb should not be in contact with the neck during a shift.
3. Left hand should remain aligned with the neck unless going past the 12th fret. Beyond the 12th fret requires some drop of the left shoulder and a slight bend in the wrist to reach higher positions and access the frets consistently.
4. Move with as little energy as possible.
5. Avoid unwanted accents when arriving in a new position by landing softly.

Use a simple chromatic scale and apply the following left-hand fingerings when ascending the fretboard: 1234, 123, 234, 12, 23, 34, and their reverse when descending the fretboard: 4321, 321, 432, 21, 32, 43.

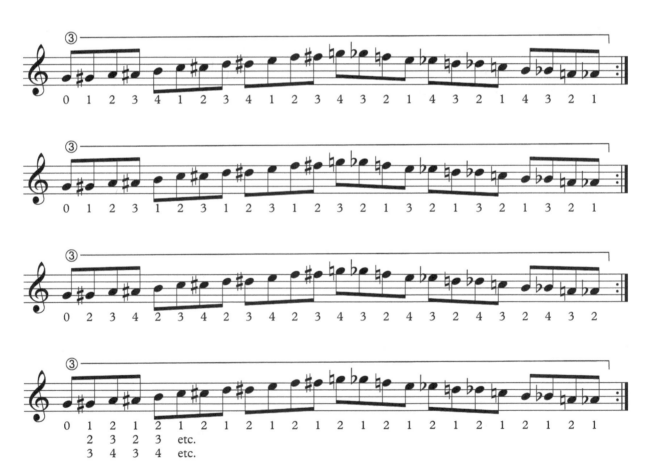

Expand the above exercises with dotted rhythms or triplets. Use the bass strings to practice minimizing left-hand shifting noise.

Open Position Major and Minor Scales

The following open position major and minor scale forms are indispensable for understanding the fretboard and discovering how to derive the most useful scale forms in higher positions on the fretboard.

Each major scale and relative minor scale has scale diagrams to help visualize the geometric shape of the scale. The melodic minor scale has both the ascending shape with the altered 6th and 7th scale degrees and the descending shape in natural minor.

When practicing the following scales, use the following fingerings (develop bold-faced fingerings first):

Rest-stroke fingerings: **im, mi, ma, am**, ia, ai, **p, ami**, ima, imam, amim, aimi

Free-stroke fingerings: **im, mi, ma, am, ia, ai, pi, pm, pa, ami**, ima, imam, amim, aimi, pmi, pami

Use the basic rhythmic groupings:

Key Points to Remember When Practicing Scales

1) Practice perfect alternation – As the finger performing the stroke moves toward its resting point, the next finger should release from its resting point to prepare the next stroke.

2) Keep everything relaxed – The only energy used is in the stroke; once it is performed, the finger should release all energy and tension. In the best-case scenario, the tension of the finger is released as the alternating finger exerts energy on the next stroke.

3) If you are still developing a technical base, spend more time on the basics – *im, ma, ia,* and finger alternation with *p* are the more important fingerings to develop, as all the others contain these basic movements.

4) Listen to your tone – If you have an ideal sound in mind, try to express it at all times. If not, experiment with tone color to explore your options, but keep in mind that the most important component of tone is clarity of attack. A beautiful and clear tone without noise before or after the pluck is ideal.

5) Feel a rhythmic pulse – Whether you are grouping 2, 3, or 7 notes, they should not all have the same intensity. Organize your groups.

6) Practice efficiency in both hands – If you can produce the same energy with less movement, you are wasting energy. Keep close to the frets and close to the strings. Proximity is your friend.

"The practice of scales solves the greatest number of technical problems in the shortest amount of time."

— Andrés Segovia

C MAJOR

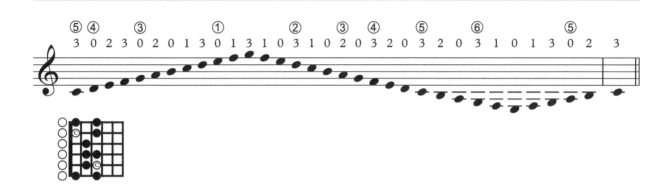

A HARMONIC MINOR

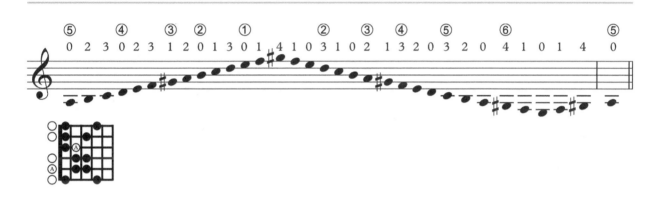

A MELODIC MINOR

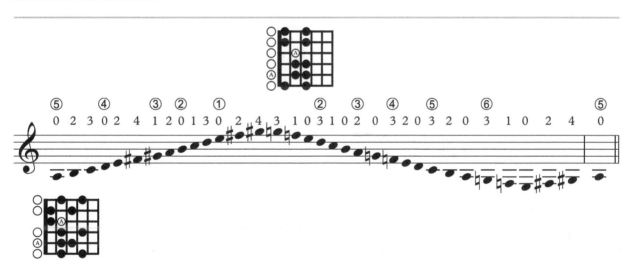

G MAJOR

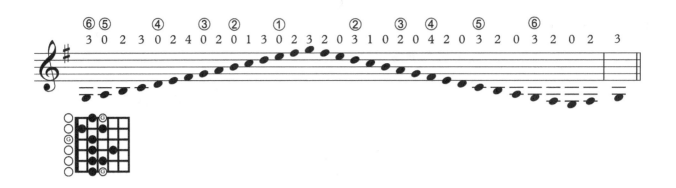

E HARMONIC MINOR

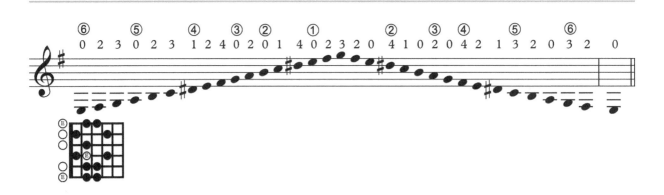

E MELODIC MINOR

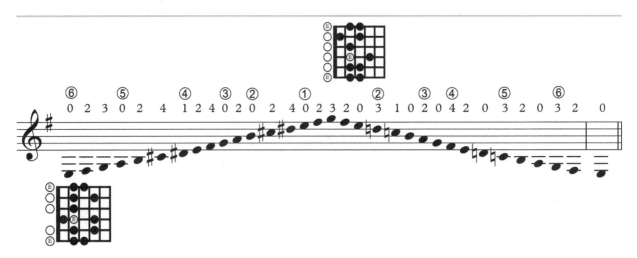

D MAJOR

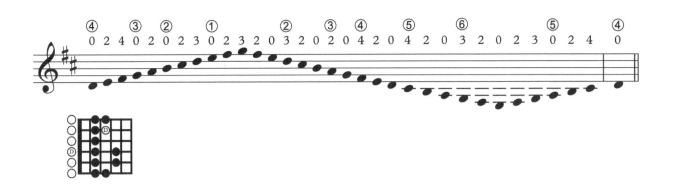

B HARMONIC MINOR

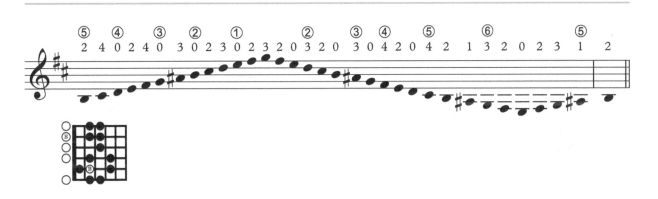

B MELODIC MINOR

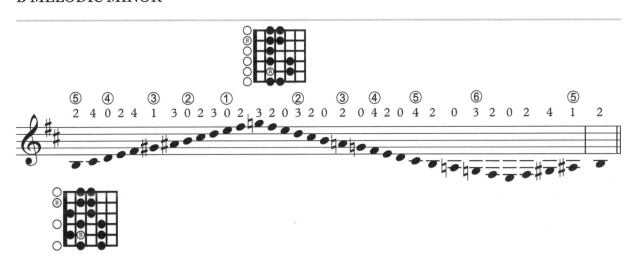

16

A MAJOR

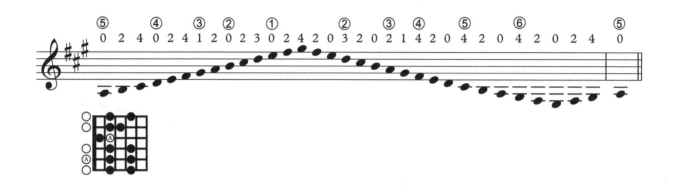

F-SHARP HARMONIC MINOR

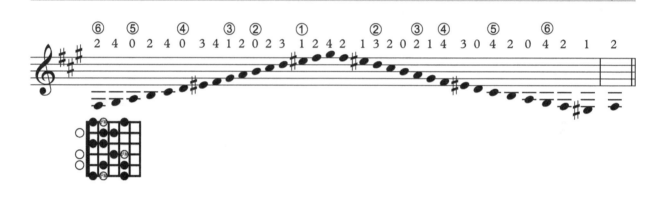

F-SHARP MELODIC MINOR

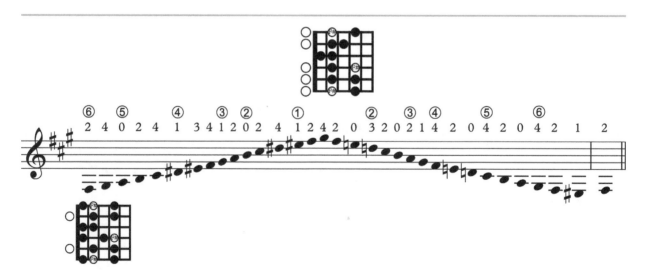

E MAJOR

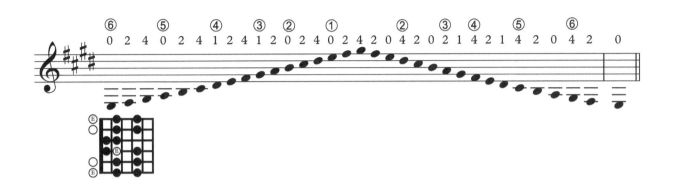

C-SHARP HARMONIC MINOR

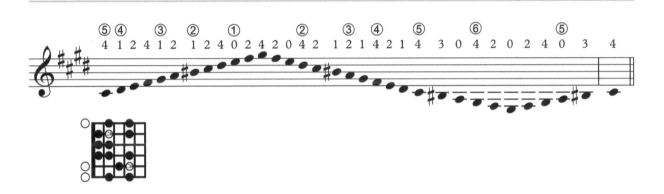

C-SHARP MELODIC MINOR

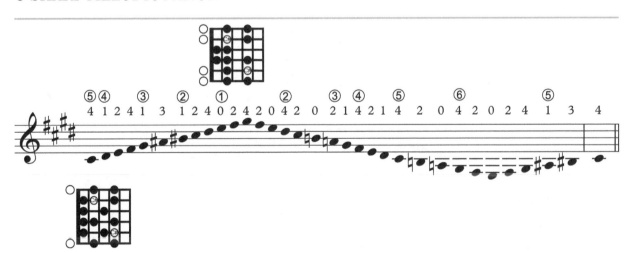

18

B MAJOR

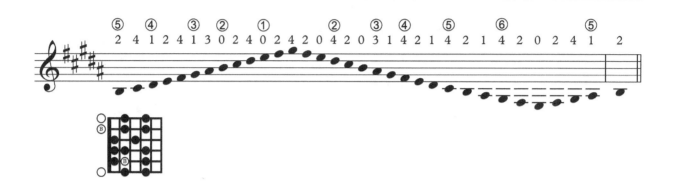

G-SHARP HARMONIC MINOR

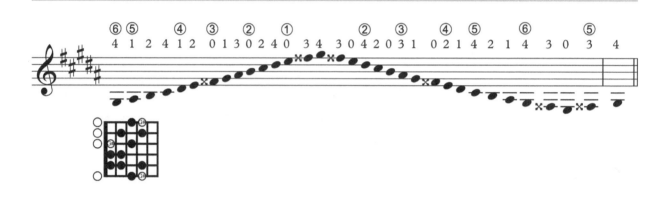

G-SHARP MELODIC MINOR

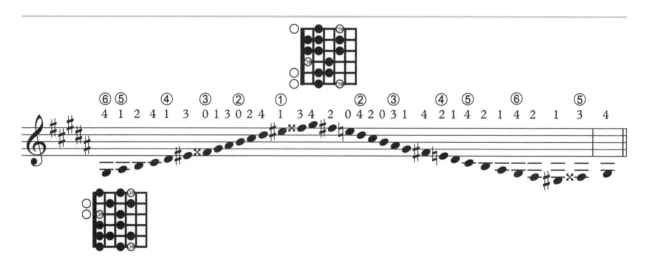

F-SHARP MAJOR

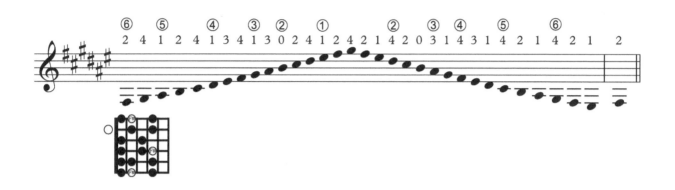

D-SHARP HARMONIC MINOR

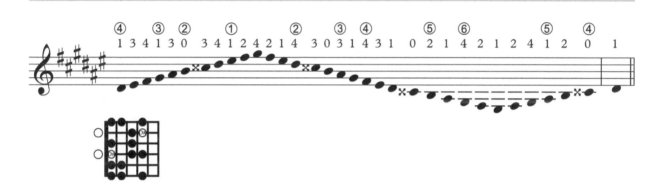

D-SHARP MELODIC MINOR

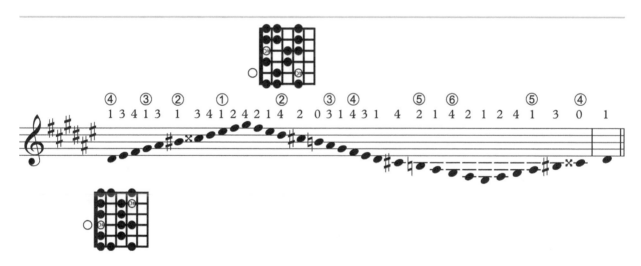

F MAJOR

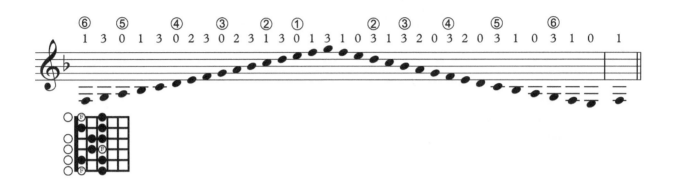

D HARMONIC MINOR

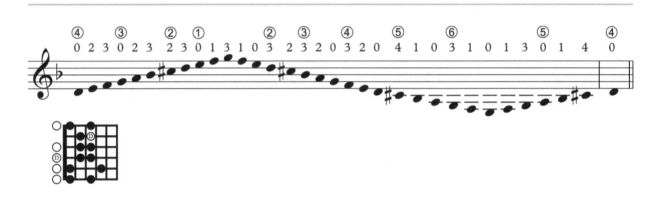

D MELODIC MINOR

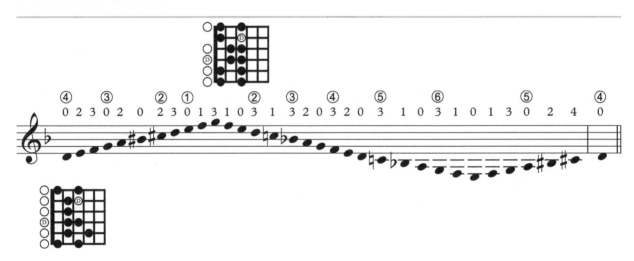

B-FLAT MAJOR

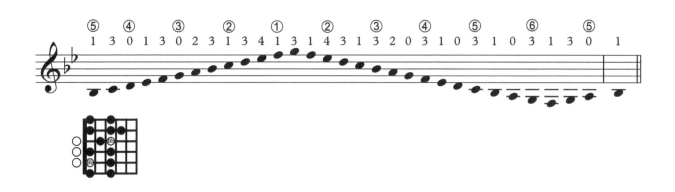

G HARMONIC MINOR

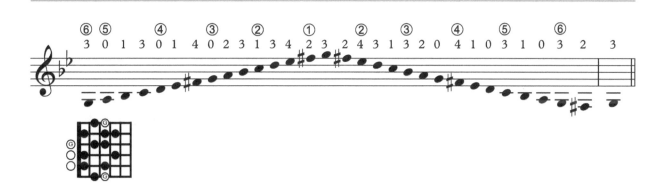

G MELODIC MINOR

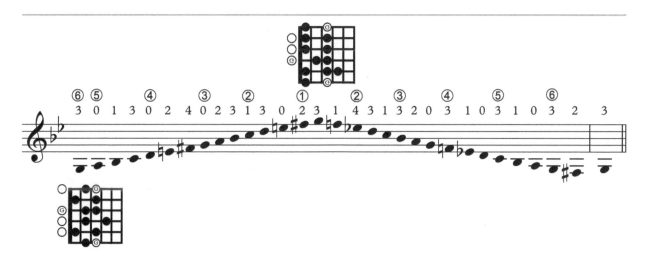

E-FLAT MAJOR

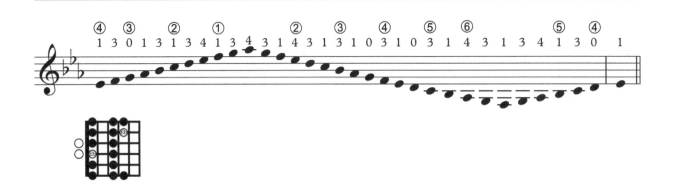

C HARMONIC MINOR

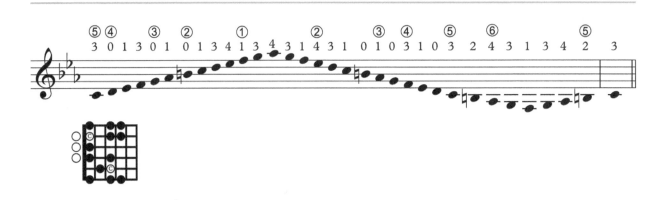

C MELODIC MINOR

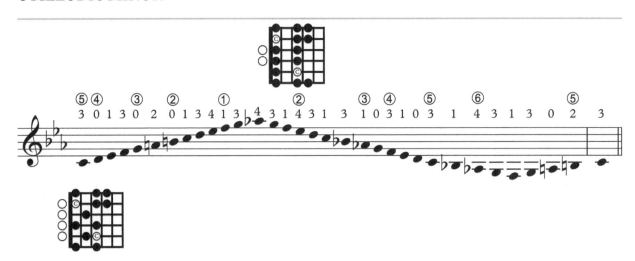

A-FLAT MAJOR

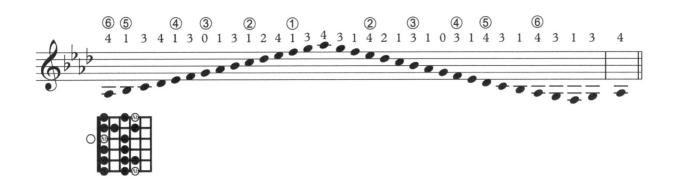

F HARMONIC MINOR

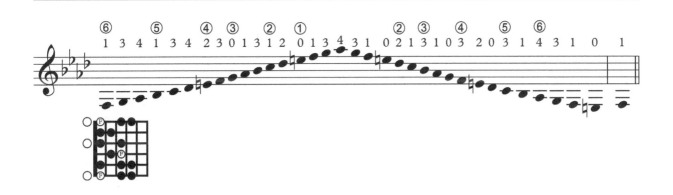

F MELODIC MINOR

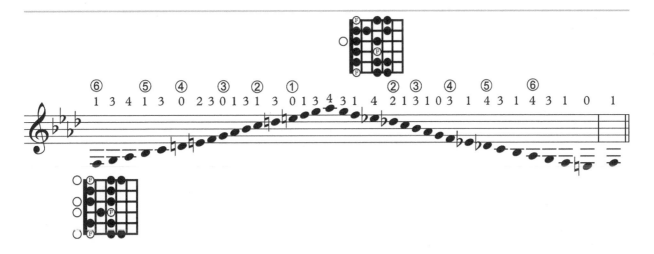

D-FLAT MAJOR

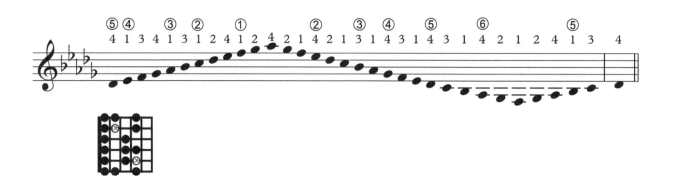

B-FLAT HARMONIC MINOR

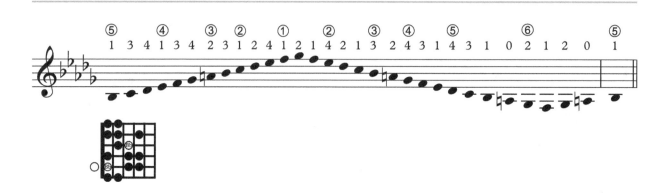

B-FLAT MELODIC MINOR

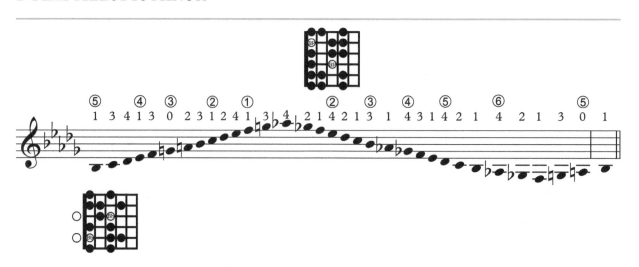

G-FLAT MAJOR

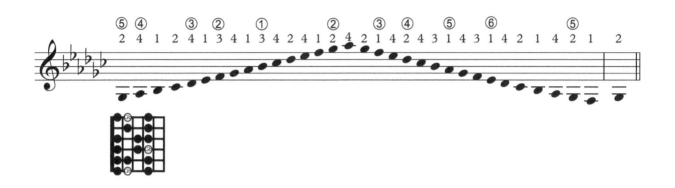

E-FLAT HARMONIC MINOR

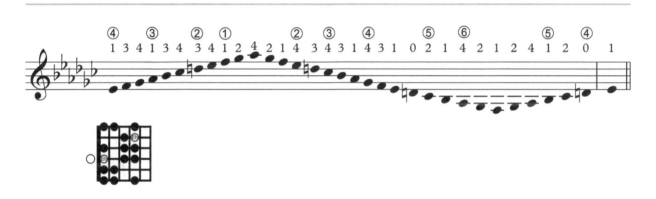

E-FLAT MELODIC MINOR

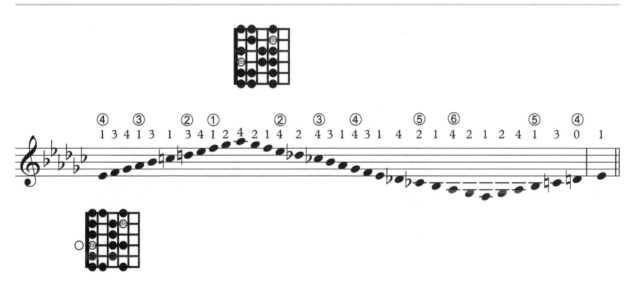

Open to Closed Position Scale Forms

If you've worked hard on memorizing the open position scales from the previous section, you essentially know scale forms that make great candidates, once shifted up along the fretboard, to create closed position forms (i.e., no open strings). Though these forms may not span the complete octaves or have the same efficient layout as the ones in the following section, it is easy to see how the most efficient closed position scales are derived.

For example, if you take the form F# Major in open position (notice there is actually only one note on an open string), shift everything up one fret (or a half step), and move the C on the second string to the third, you have an efficient and contained two-octave closed position scale form for G Major:

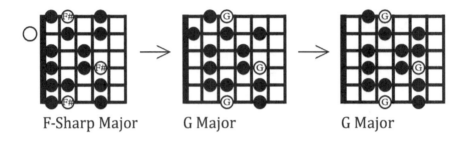

F-Sharp Major   G Major   G Major

As an exercise in fretboard and key exploration, review the open position scales, create the closed position form, and move up the fretboard one fret at a time. The following sections on closed position scale forms will make more sense after this exercise.

The following three sections are broken down into one, two, and three octave closed position scale forms. Though there are numerous forms and possibilities, the focus of this section is to provide the most useful, common, physically efficient, and practical forms encountered throughout most of the guitar repertoire. Most forms will retain a four-finger span over four frets for left hand comfort (though extensions and contractions of the fingers are necessary sometimes) and shifts are kept to a minimum. Also, if a scale form contains more than one shift, the shifts are spaced on different strings.

Knowing the most useful and efficient closed position forms is as much a valuable tool for technique development as it is for a deeper theoretical knowledge of the fretboard. For instance, if you understand a C Major closed position scale, you essentially already know a C#, D, D#, E, F, F#, G, G# (etc.) major closed position scale because you simply have to shift the whole form up or down to wherever your new starting point is.

Again, as a reminder, the melodic minor scale forms have two scale diagrams attached. The first is the ascending version of the scale and the second corresponds to the descending natural minor scale.

Closed Position One-Octave Scale Forms

Major

C Major starting on string 6

C Major starting on string 5

C Major starting on string 4

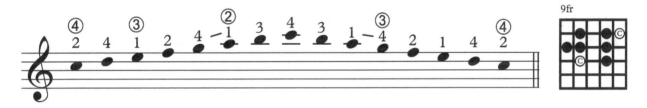

C Major starting on string 3

Harmonic Minor

C Harmonic Minor starting on string 6

C Harmonic Minor starting on string 5

C Harmonic Minor starting on string 4

C Harmonic Minor starting on string 3

29

Melodic Minor

C Melodic Minor starting on string 6

C Melodic Minor starting on string 5

C Melodic Minor starting on string 4

C Melodic Minor starting on string 3

Closed Position Two-Octave Scale Forms

The following two-octave scale forms represent the most practical forms of executing scales longer than one octave. The forms used contain a minimal number of shifts and few extensions or compressions in the left hand.

Major

Form 1

C Major starting on string 6 with finger 2

Form 2

C Major starting on string 6 with finger 4

Form 3

C Major starting on string 5 with finger 2

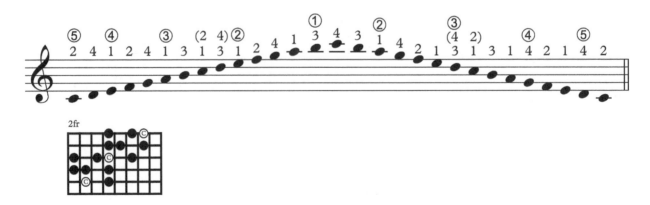

Form 4

D Major starting on string 5 with finger 4 (shift on string 1)

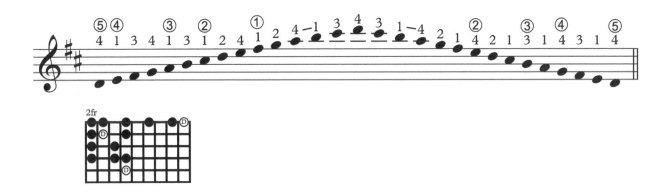

Form 5

D Major starting on string 5 with finger 4 (shift on string 3)

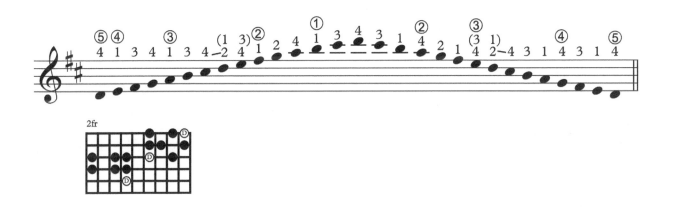

Harmonic Minor

Form 1

A Harmonic Minor starting on string 6 with finger 1

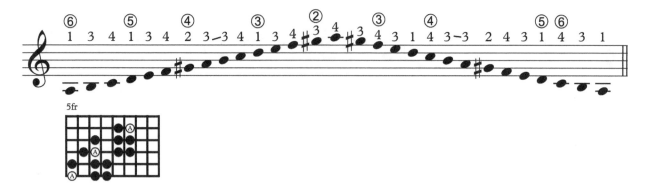

Form 2

B Harmonic Minor starting on string 5 with finger 1

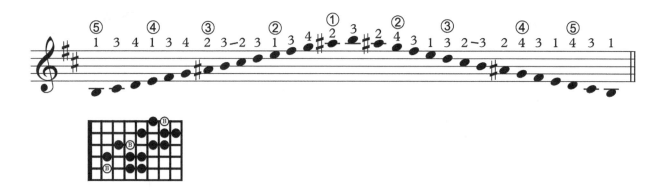

Melodic Minor

Form 1

A Melodic Minor starting on string 6 with finger 1

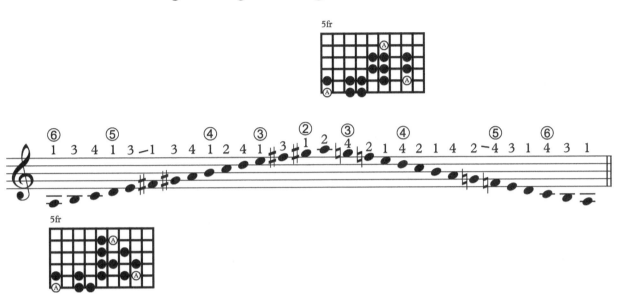

Form 2

D Melodic Minor starting on string 5 with finger 1

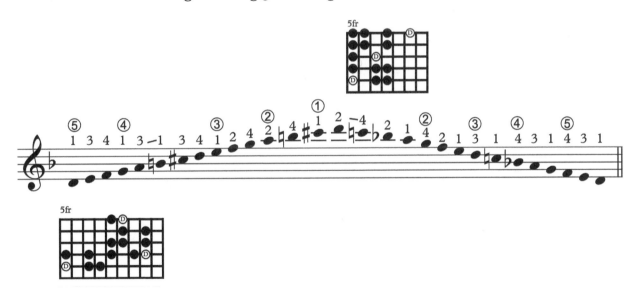

Closed Position Three-Octave Scale Forms

Major

Form 1

G Major starting on string 6 with finger 2

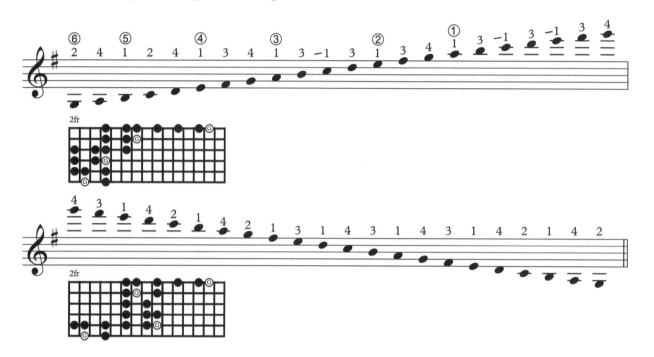

Harmonic Minor

Form 1

G Harmonic Minor starting on string 6 with finger 1

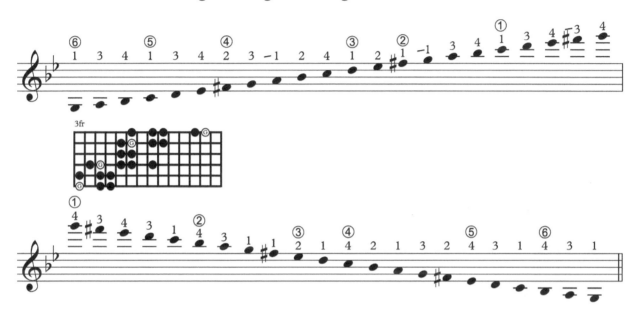

Melodic Minor

Form 1

G Melodic Minor starting on string 6 with finger 1

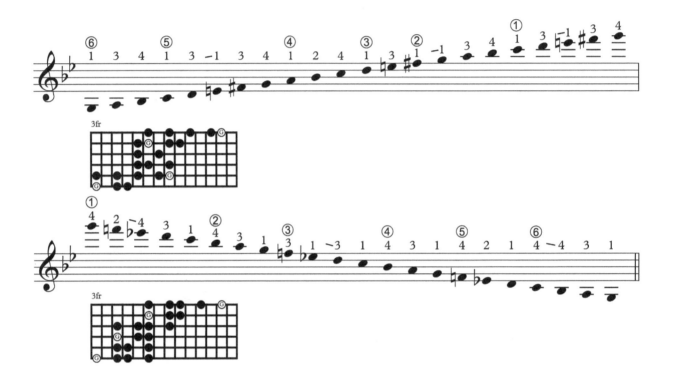

Chromatic Closed Position Scale Forms

Though not diatonic, the following chromatic scale forms are very useful in developing complete scale mastery.

C Chromatic starting on string 3

C Chromatic starting on string 4

C Chromatic starting on string 5

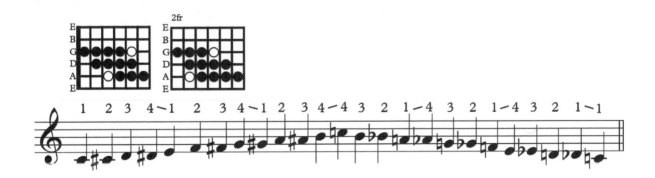

Three-Note-Per-String Closed Scale Forms

The following two-octave scale forms represent the most practical forms of executing scales where there are three notes per string. These forms are useful when trying to make triplet articulations consistent or when compound slurs would enhance the musical interpretation of the piece. The efficiency of fingering scales in this way aids in the coordination of both hands when also using three-finger patterns in the right hand (*ami, iam, mip, pmi*). The forms contain no shifts and only a few extensions or compressions in the left hand.

Major

Form 1

C Major starting on string 6 with finger 1

Note: e indicates extension between fingers 1 and 2

Form 2

C Major starting on string 5 with finger 1

Harmonic Minor

Form 1

A Harmonic Minor starting on string 6 with finger 1

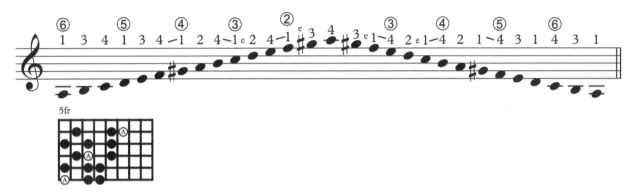

Form 2

B Harmonic Minor starting on string 5 with finger 1

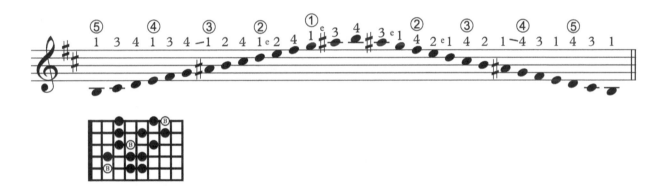

Melodic Minor

Form 1

A Melodic Minor starting on string 6 with finger 1

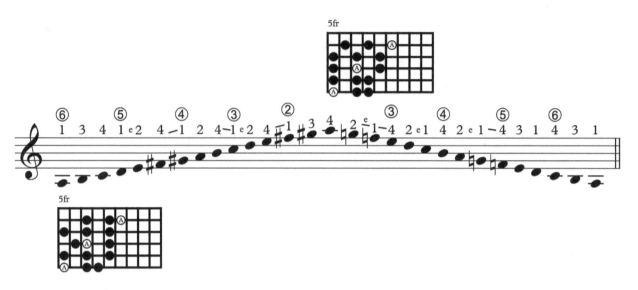

Form 2

D Melodic Minor starting on string 5 with finger 1

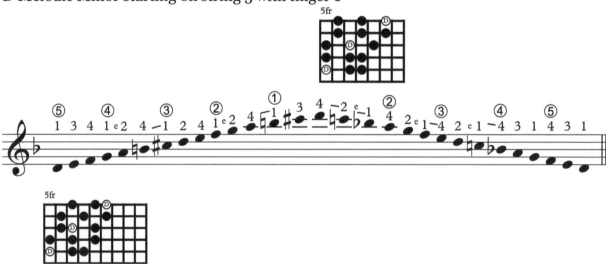

Scale Development

There are infinite ways to develop more speed, accuracy, and fluidity in your scale practice. Using rhythmic manipulation, extensor training, patterns, repeated notes, fragments, and phrasing are favorite devices. They are all explained in the next section. Once you are familiar with the various techniques, apply them to scales (or even troublesome spots) in your repertoire to either problem-solve or build a stronger foundation.

Rhythmic Manipulation

Applying rhythms to scales is an essential tool for developing speed, reflexes, mental agility, and rhythmic flexibility. Though there are many rhythms, here are the most useful ones to develop:

Two-Note Rhythms

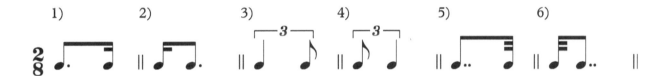

Example of the application of rhythm 1.

Example of the application of rhythm 2.

Three-Note Rhythms

Example of the application of rhythm 1.

Example of the application of rhythm 2.

Four-Note Rhythms

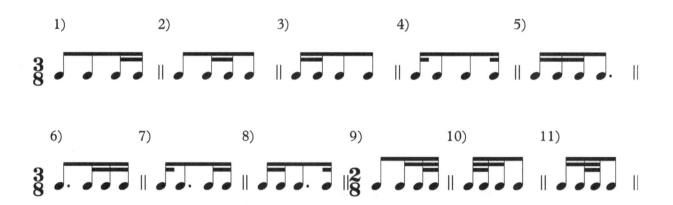

Example of the application of rhythm 5.

Example of the application of rhythm 6.

etc.

Extensor Training

Though *rasgueado* movements work the extensors extensively, the right hand benefits from specific or single-note extensor movement training. There are two ways to perform an extensor stroke with the fingers. The first way is a bit more active: place the fingernail behind the string and then flick the string with energy away from the guitar. Imagine the string is a marble and you are flicking that marble in front of the guitar. The other method is a bit more specific: place the nail above the string, push down toward the next string, and then land on it. For example, if you were going to play an extensor stroke on string 3, your nail would move through string 3 with a firm tip joint and land on string 2. Think of a reverse free-stroke that actually lands on the adjacent string.

For an extensor stroke with *p* place thumb under or below the string and then actively flick upwards (in the opposite direction of the usual stroke). Landing on the adjacent string in this case is not imperative. Flamenco guitarists would refer to the movement as *alzapua* (translated as thumbnail-raise or pick-raise). Think of an extensor stroke with *p* as a single string *alzapua*.

Practice the extensor strokes below with *i, m, a,* and *p*.

Practice the extensor strokes below with *im, am,* and *ai.*

Patterns

Though by no means extensive, use the following three- and four-note scale patterns to develop coordination and to combat awkward string-crossing moments. Combining alternating right-hand fingerings with triplets or three-finger patterns with sixteenths will further develop fluidity in your right-hand technique.

Three-Note Patterns

Step 1 – *im, mi, ma, am, ia, ai, pi, pm, pa*

Pattern 1

Pattern 2

Step 2 – *ami, ima, pmi*

Pattern 1

Pattern 2

Four-Note Paterrns

Step 1 – *im, mi, ma, am, ia, ai, pi, pm, pa*

Pattern 1

etc.

Pattern 2

Step 2 – *ami, ima, pmi*

Pattern 1

etc.

Pattern 2

Repeated Notes

To develop endurance in both the right and left hands, use repeated notes. While it may seem that repeated notes would only benefit the right hand, keeping left-hand fingers down to produce many articulated notes also demands left-hand finger strength.

The use of repeated notes also allows for some interesting coordination work. For example, playing repeated triplets (switching to a new note every three plucks) with a pair of fingers is a way to refine the balance of alternation.

Eighth Notes

Step 1 – *im, mi, ma, am, ia, ai, pi, pm, pa*

Step 2 – *ami, ima, pmi*

Triplets

Step 1 – *ami, ima, pmi*

Step 2 – *im, mi, ma, am, ia, ai, pi, pm, pa*

Sixteenth Notes

Step 1 – *im, mi, ma, am, ia, ai, pi, pm, pa*

Step 2 – *ami, ima, pmi*

Yes, you could go on to quintuplets, sextuplets, and septuplets, but spending more time strengthening foundational skills will make the more complicated and lengthy possibilities easier.

Fragments

Developing the ability to play fast or expressive fragments is arguably as important as practicing long scale forms, primarily because most repertoire contains small melodic fragments consisting of groups of three to seven notes. It is true that long scale practice pays off in Spanish repertoire (in particular the music of Joaquín Rodrigo), but among music by most other composers, from Mario Castelnuovo-Tedesco to Heitor Villa-Lobos, it is difficult to find many instances of scale runs beyond two octaves.

Using your now familiar scale forms, work on small extracts of 3–7 notes in various ways to discover which right-hand fingerings feel most comfortable and which present challenges to overcome.

Short Fragments

Step 1

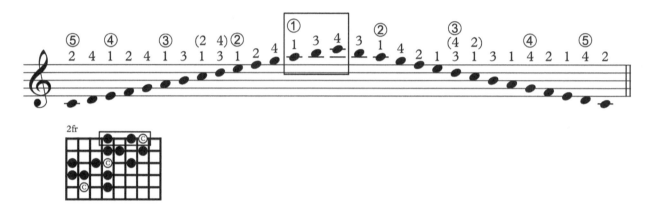

Step 2

Develop all possibilities with incremental addition of notes.

Three notes: 134, 341, 413, 431, 314, 143.
Four notes: 1341, 3413, 4134, 1343, 3431, 4313, 1434, 4341, 3414, 4143, 4314, 3143, 1431
Five notes* (my favorite): 13431, 34313, 43134, 31343, 14341, 43413, 34143, etc.

* not all possibilities listed

Longer Fragments

Step 1

Box off a larger group of notes and play in various combinations.

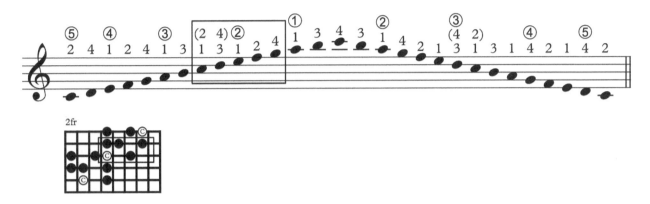

Step 2

Fiddle with the order of notes to yield and practice melodic fragments:

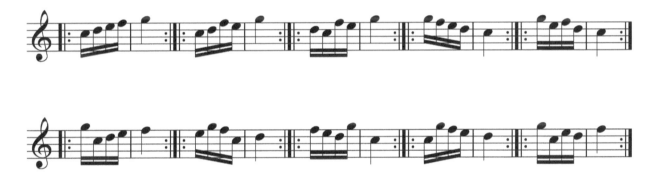

Further Development

To both the shorter and longer fragments, add slurs, articulations, accents, and character to experiment with expressivity.

Phrasing

Phrasing your scales using subtle accents and dynamics to convey note groupings is one of my favorite ways to think about music while working on scales. A slight change in articulation or accent will make your phrase move forward gracefully or plod along like an elephant. Apply the basic ideas below as a start, and then apply it to real repertoire.

Use accents to delineate a group or phrase:

Use dynamics:

Think phrasing:

Right-Hand Rules for Scales in Repertoire

Now that your scales are mastered (or are on their way), knowing how to choose wise right-hand fingering choices for your scales in the repertoire you study is important. Here are four rules that I wrote about in the Six String Journal blog and think are important to include here as well.

Note that the musical examples in this section are from Luys de Narváez's Conde Claros Variations. The third string is tuned to F#.

Rule 1

When crossing from a lower string to an adjacent higher string (i.e., string 3 to string 2):

- *im* is preferable to *mi*
- *ia* is likely preferable to *ai*
- *pi* is preferable to *ip*
- *ma* is preferable to *am*

Rule 2

When crossing from a lower string to a higher string with a string or more between them (i.e., string 4 to string 2 or string 5 to string 1)

- *ia* is preferable to *ai* and *im*
- *pm* or *pa* are likely preferable to *pi*
- *pa* is likely preferable to *pm* if the distance between strings spans three or more strings

Rule 3

Try to maintain the rules 1 and 2 throughout scales and right-hand cross-stringed fingerings. If you are unable to maintain efficient crossing you can use the following methods to ensure rules 1 and 2 are maintained.

Method 1

When playing *im* scale runs, insert *a* (ring finger) to change the direction of the fingers. Notice the use of *a* in the first box to facilitate the string crossing in the next box/boxes.

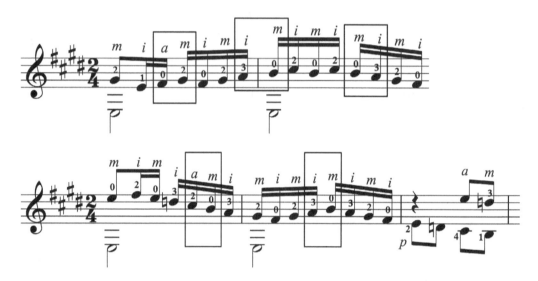

Note: The examples above require tuning the third string to F#.

Method 2

When playing *im* scale runs, insert a slur to change the direction of the fingers.

Rule 4

Do not use a slur if it is does not reflect your musical intent.

PRACTICE JOURNAL

Week 1	Notes

Week 2	Notes

Week 3	Notes

Week 4 | Notes

About the Author

Described as "a faithful interpreter of Mangore's musical art" by Alirio Diaz and as "conscientious, intelligent, musical, and technically impeccable" by Eliot Fisk, Leo Garcia is an award-winning classical guitarist, recording artist, author, and sought-after educator.

As a performer, Garcia has performed across North America, South America, and Europe, as both a soloist and as a chamber musician. As an educator, he has worked with hundreds of children and families for over 15 years through KinderGuitar. His writings have appeared in *Guitar Review*, the popular KinderGuitar blog (kinderguitar.com), and Six String Journal (sixstringjournal.com), and he has acted as jury member, performer, and lecturer at musical festivals such as the Bay Area's Junior Bach Festival, the Boston Guitar Festival, the Yale Guitar Extravaganza, and the Guitar Foundation of America's International Festival.

Leo grew up in Venezuela but left to pursue higher education in the U.S., eventually earning a B.A. in economics from Yale, an M.M. and Artist Diploma from the Yale School of Music, and a Graduate Performance degree from the New England Conservatory, before founding and developing the KinderGuitar music education system. The success of KinderGuitar led quickly to its expansion, and now with three San Francisco Bay Area locations and one in New Mexico, KinderGuitar offers training and licensing to highly qualified aspiring educators to help them create successful and sustainable music-teaching studios for children in their communities.